Writings In Ink

A collection of short poems

Advita

Writings In Ink
Copyright © 2022 by ADVITA

TABLE OF CONTENTS

DEDICATION

This is for all of you, to say that no matter how big, how small, how tall, how short, how fair, how dark, how ever you are, you can achieve anything and everything you put your mind to.

AUTHOR'S NOTE

This is me, spelt out on every word on every line in the pages of

this book. This is who I was, who I am, and who I want to be.

Please handle it with care.

Thank you.

LOST HOPE

Hope...

When snatched it can shatter your dreams and
fantasies,
Turn your world upside down,
Leave you bleeding and then question,
Who broke your imaginary crown?

Have you ever lived in fear?
Of not knowing what to expect,
If tomorrow will bring the sorrows,
Your nightmares present?

ADVITA

Because from tomorrow,
Expect the worse,
The chrysanthemums are losing colour,
As the night approaches with force.

Huddled beneath our blankets,
We cannot even pray,
For our hope and faith have shattered,
Leaving the pieces astray.

How would you feel?
To live in a world without hope,
With nothing to hold on to,
Where everything goes down a slope?

So, let's build our futures brighter,
And reach out to the light,
Because hope is the only thing we live for,
And the only thing worth the fight.

SHIMMERING HOPE

There is a silver lining
And days to start anew
There will be a new finding
And knowledge you can pursue.

When there is darkness
Reach out to the light
They will be harmless
Unless you invite.

The cuts will heal
The pain will leave
The feelings are real
As we believe.

ADVITA

The stolen tears
The broken trust
The heavy fears
Of little unjust.

The stab of grief
The aching heart
The attraction brief
Warmth miles apart.

Comfort in nothing,
Sadness swallows,
Leaving you burning,
Empty & hollow.

There is a silver lining
And days to start anew
There will be a new finding
And knowledge you can pursue.

HIM

Dear diary,

His name caught up in my throat
His smile engraved in my senses
His voice echoing in my ears
Oh, how my heart escalates.

His touch is like fire
Pulsing through my veins
My nights restless
My dreams kept at bay.

They say we're pretty close
Perhaps they don't know

ADVITA

Or don't see
Distance differs from proximity.

While I yearn for your warmth
Your muscular arms around me
You're perfectly content
Just to see me.

So, my lips have gotten used to
The ghost of my smile
My pillows damp
From the tears in my eyes.

I know you'll never see me
As more than a friend
But just know I'll be there for you
Until the very end.

Even though it will break me
To see you with someone else
A wise person once said
To love is to lose a part of yourself.

And maybe losing a part of me
Made me realise
That love is necessary
To create myself a whole again.

Even when the world is against you
No one by your side

You'll find me with your shadow
At your back at all times.

But this time not for a reason
For love or otherwise
Just simply because you're my friend
And not a lover who I can call mine.

THE FINAL POEM

I love you.
You love me.
But our journey,
Is deceit.

I don't have the courage,
Nor the strength,
To tell you to your face,
Why this would end.

So, I'm writing you this poem,
With tears in my eyes,
With a shattered heart,
And a sad smile.

Even though in my heart,
I will always know,

WRITINGS IN INK

You were the one for me,
And the only one I'd choose.

I must move on,
Because sometimes,
The person is right,
But not the time.

So, forgive me my darling,
Because I've let you down,
I'm not strong enough,
To hold on.

A lot is going on,
In my mind and elsewhere,
I can't take the burden
Of this affair.

I'll come back to you,
But I'm not asking you to stay,
Because there are more girls,
It's not worth the wait.

So, I bid you farewell,
With so much ahead of you,
Just know no one can ever love me,
The way that you do.

TIME

What is the worth of a thousand moments?
What value do seconds possess?
If we're too busy dwelling on the past?
Or living in the future?

Every second that passes by,
I only have you on my mind,
Every minute feels like infinity,
When you're not by my side.

I'm desperately waiting for the day,
When you realise,
How my love for you is eternal,
Like all of time.

And my darling,
Don't you worry,
I will wait endlessly,
For I have all eternity.

It may be a match made in heaven,
Both you and I,
But what matters is that we find each other,
Across this massive realm.

Destiny is engraved,
Our fates intertwined,
I swear to you I will,
Never leave your side.

YOU

I hate you.
I'd never have thought,
I was capable of emotion,
So deep and dark.

Your words no longer
Hold any meaning
Your promises are a
Hollow space.

Your touch now ignites
A passion of hatred
Like thorns
Pricking my skin.

Your actions speak for themselves
You are no longer who you used to be

WRITINGS IN INK

When you look at yourself in the mirror
I wonder if you see the monster you please.

Shackled to your bones
I cannot even breathe
If you've become the devil
Then I am your queen.

That's what people see
When they look at me
Not my sorrowful eyes, no,
But the crown bestowed upon me.

So, when you dragged yourself
Into a life of misery
You brought me alongside you
Only for eternity.

I hate you
For taking away my freedom
I hate you
For tying yourself to me.

And now for eternity
Hatred would pulse in my veins
Killing me before
I perish in vain.

THANK YOU

I feel like I can tell you absolutely anything and you'll understand.

I can tell you my sorrows and pain.

I can share my happiness and pride.

You wouldn't judge me like the others, no.

You'll take me by your side.

You'll be my wings when I fall.

You'll be my sun when I shine.

When the clouds fog up on a rainy day,

When lightning strikes my life.

I look at you, and you're there.

Patiently waiting for the storm to blow-by.

You remind me there will be rainbows,

When the sun shines again,

You help me plant my feet on the ground.

While my head is up there.

Thank you for being the person you are,

Thank you for staying true to yourself.

In a world filled with facades and masks,

You're the one I can count on.

WHY NOT?

In life, we look for many reasons for doing things
Always trying to justify our actions
But we need these reasons
To string us to our responsibilities
And to keep our feet grounded

But they place a burden on us
One of spite and uncertainty
The reasons make room for arguments
And riddle us full with self-doubt
Until we are so corrupted with competition
It is all that we see.

But darling, we don't need a reason to fall in love,
We don't need to answer the constant 'Why?'
We can let our imagination run free

Not held captive by
Expectations we're supposed to meet.

I love you
It's as simple as that
It's reason enough
So next time someone asks 'why?'
I'll just say, 'why not?'

Humanity is based on a change
whether it is within oneself or a societal alteration
Change is the only constant in the world
Without change, we can't grow or learn from the past.
We'll be stuck with our mistakes.

We change to adapt to different situations
Sometimes it's for survival
Others just for fun.
When we're changing for survival
It's an involuntary change before it becomes muscle
memory.

Then we depend on that change in scenarios
Transform into someone we almost don't recognize.
We uphold societal expectations
We try to alter our genes
But when we were all made different
Why change into something we weren't expected to be?

ADVITA

I love you
But it's more complicated than that
It's no longer rainbows and sunshine
Now that you've fallen into society's expectations
You've changed drastically.

We look for patterns in behavior
Try to find connections in actions
Sometimes we forge the results
Creating connections in places
They're never supposed to be.

We must remember
Each one of us is different
And to quote Einstein
We can't judge a fish
By its ability to climb a tree.

Our children are the future of the world
We mustn't let their minds be corrupted
By malicious societal expectations
We must break the stereotypes
And allow ourselves to be free.

I love you
And we can make it less complicated
If we put our differences aside
If we only stop to think
'Why ever not?'

OBSESSION

*We all have that one person who makes us feel things
no one else does.*

*You always get that sense of comfort and peace around
them.*

*You can't think of anyone else in their presence-
anything else.*

They consume you full, mind, body and soul.

*Every thought of them consumes your brain when
they're not there,*

but when you're with them, it's blank.

Like a slate wiped clean,

hundreds of thousands of words are left unspoken.

Strangling you until you can't seem to breathe.

Their eyes are a vast ocean you get lost in,

their smile teasing and wide.

You can barely sleep at night because finally,

reality is better than your dreams.

But when you do dream,

you only dream of them,

you dream of your future together.

And dream about the chaos they've created.

FREEDOM

A burden on her shoulder,
A smile on her face,
She carries on with life,
Labelled a disgrace.

Breaking free from the chains,
That tie her to her fate,
She writes her own story,
Where she isn't constantly replaced.

She walks on glass,
Yearning for the day,
When the prick doesn't sting,
And her life isn't cliché.

The story of the girl,
Who wronged her family,
Bringing shame and humiliation,
Where they lived unhappily.

But she's free now,
From the clutches of society,
From expectations and norms,
Where she isn't stabbed by anxiety

ADVITA

She's lonely now,
But she can make new friends,
Ones that will help her see clearly,
And not through a blurred lens.

It's dark before it's light,
Night before day.
Sunshine is coming,
Send the blues away.

The clouds will clear,
And you'll see the sun,
Lighting the path,
Where you can run.

With wind in your hair,
Nothing holding you back,
The burden on your shoulder,
You can finally unpack.

ILLUSION

In your reflection,
What do you see?
Do you see grace and charm,
And all that you can be?

Or do you see a wreck?
Hopes and dreams destroyed,
Where once there was a beauty,
Now it has been spoiled.

Not by the scars she has on her face,
Not by the bags under her eyes,
But by the way we've defined beauty,
With all the fables and the lies.

Not every girl can be Cinderella,
Kind and selfless and pretty,
We need to fight for what we want,
Before we're thrown out of the city.

ADVITA

Beauty is an illusion,
Don't expect me to trust you,
When you prefer layers of makeup,
Over the scars on my face you drew.

If an artist doesn't like the portrait,
He worked day and night to make,
He'll spend days and nights more,
To rectify his mistake.

Alas, you can't change the strokes,
Of pain and hurt and grief,
But you can stop painting a perfect picture,
On an already perfect reef.

Don't tell me I'm not beautiful,
That I don't have a symmetrical face,
Just because you are deluded by society,
Doesn't mean you can snatch my grace.

WILL THE SUN EVER SHINE?

The clouds hung low,
Weeping on humans,
What is this place?
What are these ruins?

Four corners,
Four walls,
I was forced to listen,
To the horrendous squalls.

It screamed and cried,
No one ever seemed to listen,
They are all too busy,
With their own vision.

I was on cloud nine,
Now I am on a deserted island,

ADVITA

My world changed so quickly,
That I sit frightened.

The sun stopped shinning,
I haven't moved an inch,
This strange room before me,
Has brought me to flinch.

The mere thoughts of smiles and laughter,
Cause a deep aching inside,
I don't want to face the world,
when a part of me has died.

Sadness swallows me whole,
And I sit here thinking,
Why doesn't anyone stop to wonder,
Why am I still sinking?

I cling to the last of my sanity,
For the hope of a better tomorrow,
When maybe the sun will shine,
And I'll be free of my sorrow.

CHILDHOOD

My childhood,
Is a fever dream,
Leaving me with memories,
Flowing like a tranquil stream.

The days passed in a blur,
Filled with laughter and colours,
Days runnin' around,
And hidin' under the covers.

Afraid of the dark,
Of the monster underneath the bed,
Not knowing the real danger,
Lurks inside my head.

Watchin' cartoons,
Playin' games,
Not knowin' when,
Everything went up in flames.

Livin' in a fairy world,
Waitin' for my prince,
Dreams caught in the wind,
Hope doesn't wince.

Passion and purpose,
Written in stone,
Leaving oneself,
A mere clone.

Duty above all else,
Suppressin' desire,

ADVITA

How do I look at myself in the mirror,
When I'm a pathological liar.

My childhood is a fever dream,
Filled with fables and lies,
Everything is written in stone,
And not one goddamn surprise.

ALPHABETS

Absence

Your presence has always been oxygen in my life,

Vital for me to live, survive,

Yet it's choking me,

I'm dead while alive,

Caged while free,

I dream about your absence,

Yet, have nightmares about your presence.

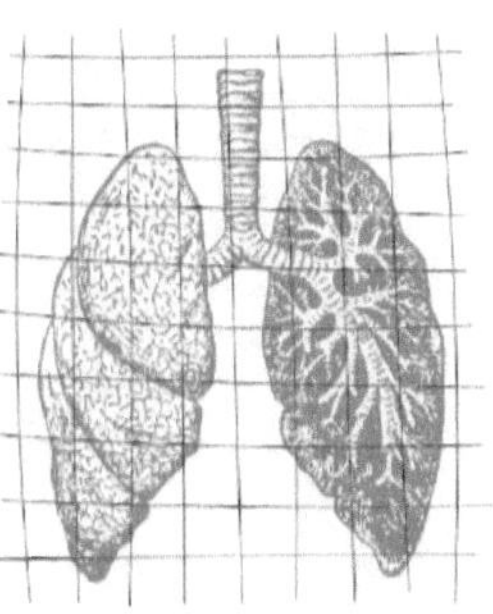

Betrayal

Promises mean nothing to me,

You promised me the world,

I laugh looking around the ashes,

All you gave me were gashes,

So deep they cut my bone,

Distracting me as you take my throne.

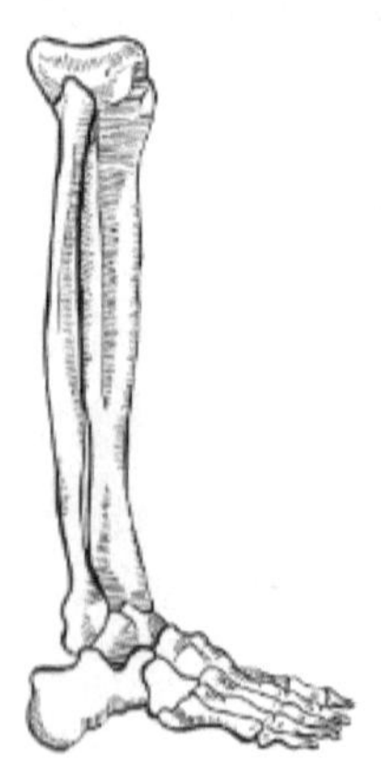

Chaos

There is a fire raging inside you,

Contrasting the waves in your heart,

A constant battle between light & dark,

Sometimes you get burned,

But that doesn't stop you,

Every incident is a lesson learned.

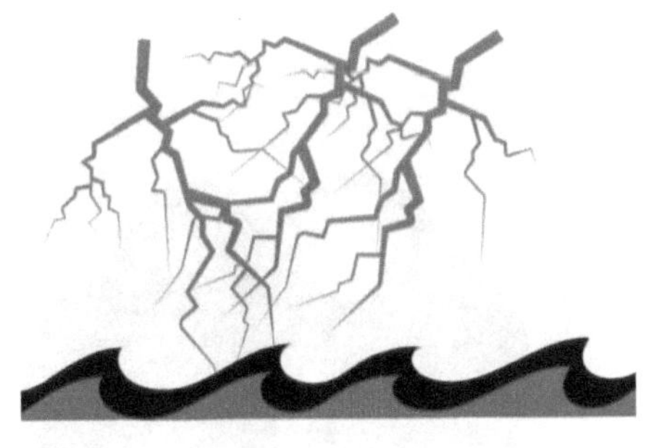

Dreams

What are dreams?

Are they just random firing of neurons?

Or are they something deeper?

Do dreams give you peace at night?

Or are they the ones that leave you with fright?

Everyone has dreams,

But only some can muffle their screams.

Euphoria

Your smile is so bright it lights up my heart,

The adrenaline I get on roller coasters,

Is nothing in comparison to talking to you,

You reign your life like a painter with a canvas,

All the while creating a masterpiece of art,

You are the definition of a sky so blue,

In the sea of the world, you will always stand apart.

Freedom

In a world shackled by expectations,

Of what society thinks of us,

You smile and live carefree,

Why frown when tomorrow isn't a guarantee?

It's better to live on your own terms,

To have regrets you can call your own,

Instead of dreaming of a time and place,

Where all your mistakes you would erase.

Galaxies

Brighter than the moon,

Radiant like the sun,

Your twinkling eyes,

Rival the stars,

The universe exists within you,

When you look up at the skies,

Everything will play along to your tune.

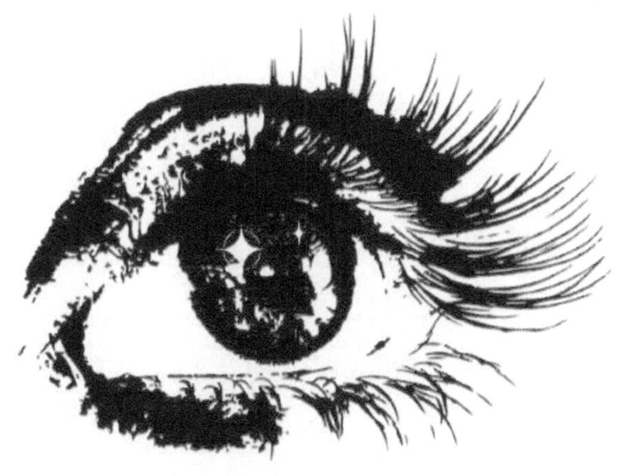

Harmony

Orchestrating your life,

Ensuring each note is precise,

Each misstep a rhythm,

Part of the design,

Sonnets of resilience,

Shadows and sunlight in stories untold,

Etched in time both black and white,

The melody of your life,

A symphony so bright.

Infinity

In this universe,

There is love and hate,

Kindness and cruelty,

but at the end of the day,

It's only you that has given me infinity,

Two moments spent in your presence,

Are enough to last a lifetime,

I'm content as I sit here,

& make words rhyme.

Justice

What goes around comes around,

Some may call it karma,

Others call it fate,

In the essence of right & wrong,

Justice sings a poetic song,

We carry our own weight,

And weave our own life,

Sowing seeds of kindness,

Or brewing potions of malice.

Kaleidoscope

You are a source of inspiration,

A beacon of light,

Your presence brings warmth to every room,

And in your laughter, melodies bloom,

A symphony of joy,

Chasing away the gloom,

Your journey unfolds like a captivating tale,

Each chapter adorned with resilience

& kaleidoscopic detail.

There are multiple ways to get lost,

Lost in thought, a labyrinth of the mind,

Or lost in space, where stars are tossed,

But I feel the saddest of them all,

Would be to lose your sense of self,

In the noise of conformity, don't sway,

Be the melody in your own unique way,

For being ordinary is the worst insult of all.

Mystery

In lines I dance,

With words I play,

A tapestry of thoughts,

Both night and day,

Rhymes and rhythms,

In my sway,

Unlock my secret,

What am I? Do say.

Neptune

In the cosmic sea,

forgotten and vast,

The last of every line,

A memory cast,

In a watery palace,

Neptune's throne,

With trident in hand,

His rule is known.

Oblivion

Escaping reality's constant reminder of mortality,

In pages of books, she is immortal,

A creator in realms of her own,

She weaves dreams of a life, normal,

In her crafted worlds, she stands alone.

Paradox

You light up the room by burning yourself,

The embers of your soul a contrast to your icy blaze,

People think you are their sun,

Shining bright and free,

But you are darkness undone,

A thundering storm in the middle of the sea.

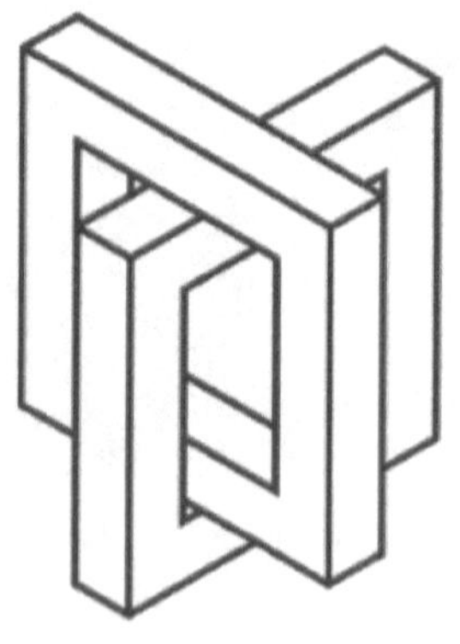

Quests

Through uncharted lands,

Where mysteries are sown,

A compass of questions guides the way,

A quest for truths, a pursuit so bold,

We find treasures more precious than gold,

In the whispers of endless trails,

Where destinies blend,

The lost find themselves,

In a circle that has no end.

Rebellion

Changing the script, writing our fate,

The hand dealt to us,

Is our greatest bait,

As our stories unfold,

Break the mold,

Let the pen dance, let the voices soar,

Changing the script, rewriting our fate,

Our journey, our choice,

Welcome to the rebel's gate.

Shadows

Haunted by our past,

Demons of our nightmares,

With darkness entwined,

A dance in the shadows of the subconscious mind,

Echoes of yesterdays,

Whispers of regret,

When all we can do is live with the threat.

Torment

Our havens are powerful,

They provide hope in desperate times,

And equally destructive despair in others,

The power we give to other people,

To dictate how our life would be,

Why obsess over 15 seconds?

When 86,385 seconds of our day is free?

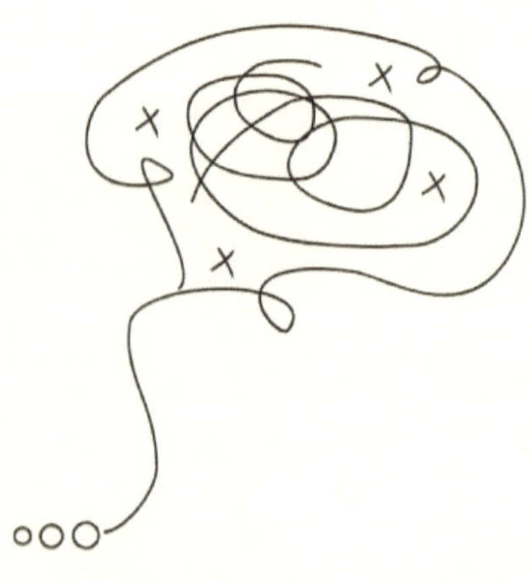

Utopia

People spend decades trying to find perfectionism,

And still fail,

In the quest for flawlessness,

A mirage on an ever-shifting trail,

For in the quirks and the scars you bear,

Lies the beauty that's uniquely rare,

In a world full of imperfections,

You are Utopic.

Valiant

Triumphing every challenge,

Her story yet untold,

A soldier of resilience,

Of heart, blood & soul,

No capes flutter,

No masks conceal,

Yet, your impact, so profound and real,

You are our hero in a dupatta.

Wonderland

A place where winter's crazed,

Alice twirls completely dazed,

Intoxicated with a dream of her own,

With crazy tales & mysteries sown,

In its enchanting embrace,

Through the looking glass,

A world unknown,

Where reality blurs & wonders are sown.

Xenogeny

A rose in the wild,

A light in the dark,

Curious glances,

A radiant spark,

In the garden of oddities,

It takes its stand,

Not a standard glow,

Nor a conventional hue,

Yet, a vibrant show.

Yesterday

We spend eternity contemplating the past,

Agonizing over moments we can't change,

Our life bleeds on,

Yet we're stuck long after it has passed,

Why do we drown ourselves in the misery of what if?

Why do we always want to look back?

Our eyes are in front for a reason,

So, don't bother looking back.

As quickly as people put you up,

They can put you down quicker,

Don't let others define your self-worth,

Don't conform to their flicker,

As quickly as they crown you in the light,

Judgment in shadows and darkness,

Will cloud your sight.

TREASURES

Surrounded by treasures of all kinds,
You always want more,
When will you learn,
The greatest treasures are the ones you ignore.

When mom sets the dinner table,
When dad asks for help at the store,
You say you're too busy,
To even show up at the door.

Your seat is empty,
You're locked up in your room,
An actress in your own world,
Always wearing a different costume.

A new day, A new dress,
You've changed beneath the mask,
But how do we know who you are,
When all you do is scream when we ask?

Maybe when we're gone you'll realise,
The importance of family,
To keep your friends close,
Or you'll live your ever after, unhappily.

THORNS

You notice beauty in monsters,
Kindness in storms,
But when it comes to you,
All you notice are the thorns.

When will you learn,
You deserve love too,
So, cheer up,
And stop feeling so blue.

Who cares if you have thorns,
The most beautiful poems have been written,
About storms, monsters & roses,
In which thorns are celebrated, not hidden.

So, here's to your thorns,
Because they make a part of you,
And whoever criticizes a rose,
Isn't good enough to pursue.

You notice beauty in monsters,
Now you'll notice it within,
Beauty is in the eye of the beholder,
Take a mirror to begin.

MOONLIGHT

She stood out in a crowd,
Her beauty rivalled the stars,
What the sunlight hid,
Were the depth of her scars.

She preferred the shadows,
Where she could find solace in the dark,
For they wouldn't judge her,
Or laugh at the mark.

The marks that she was told to hide,
Because they were a symbol of her weakness,
Something to be ashamed of,
And not a testament to her uniqueness.

Hiding beneath layers of clothes,
Beneath heaps of make-up,
Desperately waiting until,
From this dream she'll wake up.

Only her diary knew her deepest thoughts,
Only the moonlight gave her enough strength,
To present herself bare,
As an enticing reward for death.

ADVITA

In silence she screamed,
In laughter she concealed,
Her tears blending in the rain,
Acting as her shield.

A knife held close,
A silent plea,
Bleeding through the numb pain,
Hoping death is a mercy.

SPACE

A bounce in her walk,
A smile on her face,
Present here right now,
But she's in space.

Walking amongst the stars,
Her head in the clouds,
Let's escape to paradise,
Away from the crowds.

The earth orbits the sun,
The closest star it could find,
The one that shines the brightest,
Even when left behind.

She has hope despite it all,
A smile that masks her disappointment,
Cause why wallow in misery,
When we could bask in enjoyment?

Enchanté Monsieur,
Her voice rang out,
A melody so sweet,
Leaving you with no doubt.

MIND

Another year passes by,
Leaving pain and happiness behind,
You tell me it's still Monday,
Was that all in my mind?

How do seconds bleed into hours?
How does time stand so still?
My mind is in total chaos,
Yet, the world moves by at will.

Moments feel like memories,
I know I should remember,
The calendar says it's May
But I'm still stuck in December.

The Christmas lights in the corner,
Light up parts of my heart,
I had kept hidden away,
Afraid they'd tear me apart.

The echoes of laughter and joy,
From seasons long gone by,
Resurface in this quiet room,
Where time seems to lie.

CARBON DIOXIDE

Just keep breathing,
How can I?
When the Carbon dioxide in my lungs,
Turns my blood acid,
And leaves my eyes dry.

Suffocated by expectations,
By being the object of perfection,
Never truly living,
Nor finding a connection.

Surrounded by shadows,
In the voices and the lies,
The media's cruel depiction,
Of what they idealize.

I don't fit in conventional standards,
So I create my own,
Where uniqueness is celebrated,
And expectations are overthrown.

I seek pure air,
Far from this strife,
Inhaling the oxygen,
I reclaim my life.

ADVITA

ACKNOWLEDGEMENTS

Wow, you made it to the end!
Thank you so much for taking out the time to read little pieces of my life.

I'd like to thank my parents for supporting me through this journey.

I am deeply grateful to my mother, whose unwavering support always pushes me to put my best foot forward.

Thank you, dad, your aspirations for my success drive me forward.

To my sister, who fills my heart with love and inspiration.

This is for my friends, for inspiring me to pursue and persevere: Fatema, Kush, Lahek, Soumya, & Tanvi.
Thank you from the top, middle, and bottom of my heart.

Thank you, family, for all the love and support I've got my whole life in everything I do!